A Howl

Written by Marie Gibson
Illustrated by Kelvin Hawley

Contents

Chapter One

"Peli?" Arnya whispered in a dejected voice. "When are they coming back?"

Peli glanced up at his sister from the embers of the dying fire. "Soon," he told her, knowing that what he said was a lie.

"We'll be back before the next sunrise," their father had said, but the sun had risen three times since then, and their parents hadn't returned. As Peli stared at the third stone, the one he had laid out for today's sunrise, his stomach turned over with fear. Something terrible must have happened to keep them away this long.

"Look after the fire, Peli," was the last thing his father had told him. "And stay out of the forest." He had picked up his lance and his club and, barefooted, walked ahead of their mother down the narrow cliff track. The worn skin pouch containing his cutting tools swung at his waist.

Peli and Arnya had watched them from the cave entrance until they disappeared into the forest.

"I'm hungry and I'm cold," Arnya complained, interrupting her brother's thoughts. It was late afternoon, and they faced another night alone. She shivered as a dark bank of cloud rolled up from behind the western mountains. It blotted out the sunlight that had been shining on the treetops below. More rain showers were on the way. This was the third wet day in a row. Arnya pulled the skin of the bear they had killed last autumn close around her thin body.

It had been an evening like this when the bear had tried to take the cave for its long winter sleep. The fire had died down to a few embers and the family went into the forest to gather wood.

They were on their way back to the cave when sharp-eyed Peli spotted the bear. It was sitting on its haunches at the entrance to the cave, taking no notice of the dying fire. Bears, with their vicious claws and great strength, were afraid of nothing.

It was only their father's cleverness and courage that helped them to win back the cave. First, he shouted to attract the bear's attention. He pelted it with rocks until it roared with rage, then ran back into the forest, with the bear chasing behind him. He led it towards a pit they had dug to trap a wild boar, and ran lightly across the sticks that covered it. From the far side, he taunted the bear and threw more rocks at it.

The bear charged! Its great weight smashed through the fragile sticks and sent it crashing into the pit. Then Father, Mother, and Peli had stabbed the beast with lances and spears until it was dead.

"I wish Mother and Father hadn't gone." Arnya was still complaining.

"They didn't want to go," Peli told her again. How many times had he said that? "They went hunting because we must have meat."

"But why did they go so far?"

"Because there's nothing to hunt around here. Not since the summer. You know how hungry we have been." He thought about the rabbit and the small pile of nuts and berries they had had to last until their parents came back. Only the rabbit bones were left. No wonder they were hungry.

"I wish they had taken us with them."

"You know why they didn't!" Peli was starting to sound impatient. But, as soon as Arnya pulled her foot back out of sight under the bearskin, he felt ashamed of himself. She hated that foot. It was smaller than the other one, and the toes didn't bend properly. When she walked, she limped. She could never have kept up on a long journey.

Peli still remembered the night his sister was born. It was eight summers ago, when he was six. At that time, they had lived with five other families, and Peli had had friends to play with. But a child who wasn't born perfect was bad luck.

"An evil omen," the women said as they stared down at the baby. They shook their heads and turned away. There wasn't the usual feasting and celebration for the birth. The other children were not allowed to come near the baby, nor were they allowed to play with Peli.

"It's a sign that there will be floods – or maybe drought. The animals will disappear. The hunting will be poor. We will all suffer." The men muttered and shuffled their feet in the soft sand. One of them picked up his spear and tested its weight, glancing at the others through narrowed eyes.

Peli's mother was ready for them. She tucked the baby under a ledge at the back of the cave. "Get behind me," she told Peli.

Together, holding spears and hunting clubs ready, Peli's parents stepped between the baby and the men. His father was taller and stronger than the other men, but Peli knew it was the savage fury in his mother's eyes that made them slink away. If it came to a battle, the others' larger numbers would win, but many would die in the struggle.

For six days, Peli's mother kept his baby sister hidden in the back of the cave. Then, early one morning, while the others were still asleep, they had crept away to look for a new home. Zye, their father's younger brother, went with them. They took a torch so that they would have fire, and they walked for many days until they found this cave.

Maybe those women had been right about Arnya bringing bad luck, Peli thought. He remembered the day Zye and his father went off on a hunt, but only one of them came back.

"A leopard," his father said, staggering in under the weight of the spotted animal. "It surprised Zye by the waterhole. He didn't have a chance."

It wasn't until the cat's body dropped onto the floor of the cave that Peli saw the claw slash on his father's shoulder. His mother wrapped the wound in special leaves, but that night his father kept them awake with his groaning. It was two days before he was strong enough to bring back Zye's body. He never got over the loss of his brother.

Glancing across at the heavy stone marking the place where they had buried his uncle under a pile of rocks, Peli remembered how Zye was always laughing and teasing, telling Peli what a great hunter he would be. But it didn't happen like that.

At first, they had said that Arnya wasn't old enough to come, so Peli had to stay behind to look after her. Then, when she was old enough, they said that, if a fierce animal turned on them, Arnya's bad foot would make her too slow to escape. His father kept saying, "You can go next time, Peli." But it was always "next time".

One night, Peli was listening when he should have been sleeping. He heard his mother say, "There has been good hunting lately. Do you think the bad luck is over, now that the leopard has killed your brother?" But, as far as Peli was concerned, the bad luck had grown stronger.

"If Zye had lived, he would have made Father take me with them," Peli muttered. His mother could have looked after Arnya. All the same, he had to admit that there had been plenty of meat, as well as berries and nuts from the forest.

That was until last summer. Since then, there had been no rain, and the sun shone bright and hot. The streams dried up. So did the waterholes where animals came to drink. They had had almost no meat – only a hare once, and sometimes a bird that Father got with a stone from his sling.

Then, three days ago, only hours after their parents had left, black clouds gathered over the mountains, and big raindrops hissed on the hot stones around the fire. After that, one rain shower had followed another. The waterhole would be full by now. The animals would soon come there to drink. Peli wished with all his heart that his parents had waited.

Despairing, Peli gathered up the last armful of sticks and tossed them onto the fire. The embers fed on the bark and dried leaves. They flickered then flared, lighting up the dark-haired boy in his deerskin tunic that was already too small for him. Arnya's shadow loomed large on the cave wall, reminding him again of the bear. Only a blazing fire would keep the next one away.

"I'm going for more wood," Peli announced.

"But Father said to stay out of the forest."

12

"I know, but Father isn't here. Do you want the fire to go out?"

"No," Arnya muttered as she struggled to her feet. "But, if you're going, I am, too."

"No. You stay here. You're too slow."

"I'm not," Arnya insisted. "I can carry some wood, too. Anyway, you know what Father said, 'Never go into the forest alone.'"

Peli hesitated, undecided. What if something happened to her? His mother and father would never forgive him – that's if they ever came back. But Arnya was right, no one should go into the forest alone.

"All right," he said at last. "You light a torch."

"But it's not dark yet. And we're not to waste the torches."

"I know that. It's in case we meet up with some dangerous animal." Their father had hunted down the leopard that killed Zye, but Peli knew there would be others. "The torch will keep it away."

Arnya dropped the bearskin and limped into the cave. When she came back, she had an empty bag tied around her waist. In her hand, she carried

13

a heavy stick. Bark soaked with bear fat was wrapped around one end. She poked it into the flames until the fat spluttered and crackled, then flared up, sending the children's shadows leaping behind them into the darkness of the cave.

"Come on then." Peli had been scanning the edge of the forest. Except for the breeze that always stirred the tops of the tallest trees at this time of day, everything was still.

Peli scrambled down the zigzag path to the bottom of the cliff. If he didn't hurry, he might be too scared to go. Arnya followed him just as fast, in spite of her foot. A few minutes later, they had reached the scattered trees at the edge of the forest, but the ground there was bare. They had already gathered all the fallen branches. They would have to go further. Their eyes searched into the darkness of the forest itself.

Neither of them looked back. They didn't see the dark shape that crept around the side of the hill towards the cave.

Chapter Two

Arnya and Peli hurried some distance through the forest before stopping. A strong wind had blown the night before and dead sticks littered the ground.

Peli took the torch from his sister and rammed the pointed end into the ground, then piled stones around it to make sure it stayed upright. While he set about gathering an armful of wood, Arnya stood staring into the lower branches of a nearby tree. "Don't just stand there," he ordered. "Help me pick up these sticks."

Arnya ignored him. She moved closer to the tree and began parting its leaves with her hands.

Suddenly, Peli was startled by a rustling in the branches above Arnya's head. Something was up there. "Look out!" he yelled, leaping back.

Arnya flattened herself on the ground as a large bird swooped down. Its harsh cawing threatened them as it swerved away, its wings beating through the cooling air. Arnya stared after it until it disappeared, then she stood up and returned to searching the leaves. "Only a crow," she said with relief. "I wish we could catch it."

"What are you doing there?" Peli demanded, embarrassed that he had been scared by a bird.

"Gathering these nuts." Arnya pulled some from the tree and tucked them into her bag. Peli was tempted to drop his firewood and get some nuts for himself. He was so hungry. But Arnya was hungry, too, and she wasn't eating. He knew she would wait to share with him back at the cave, the way their parents always did.

As they reached the bottom of the cliff, the sun slipped behind the hill above their cave and they were suddenly chilled. It wasn't only from the drop in temperature, but also from the fear of spending another night alone.

Peli dropped his wood outside the cave. "We'll have to get more," he said, staring at the little heap of sticks. "This won't last until morning."

"Now?" Arnya had panted up behind him. She bent to hide her bag of nuts under a rock.

Peli nodded. "Come on." He grabbed the torch and set off again, glancing over his shoulder to make sure Arnya was following.

This time, there was no gathering nuts. They both picked up as much wood as they could carry and hurried out of the forest. They knew about the animals that came out at night – the big cats and the wolves. Leopards sprang on their prey from the trees above. Wolves drifted through the forest like shadows. Both animals were meat eaters, and short of food, too. By the time the children reached the safety of their cave, Peli was imagining he could hear the coughing snarl of the leopard or the click of wolves' claws on the rocks.

Squatting by the fire, Arnya watched Peli break a few twigs from one of the branches. He poked them into the embers and blew gently. Smoke spiralled upwards and tiny flames flickered. He lay larger sticks across the twigs and blew again. Then they both sat back on their heels and stretched their hands out to the warming flames.

"Now," said Arnya, when she began to feel warmer. "Food." She rolled back the rock, untied the bag, and emptied the nuts onto a flat rock by the fire. Peli wedged one in a crevice, picked up a stone, and cracked the shell. His black-rimmed fingernails prised it apart, revealing the pale, juicy nut.

"Yours," he said, passing it to Arnya. Then he cracked another for himself and chewed the sweet nut inside. He went on cracking nuts and handing every other one to his sister until they were all finished. He could have eaten more, but the awful gnawing in his stomach was gone. Somehow, somewhere, they would have to find more food for tomorrow, and the next day, and the next.

Peli thought about the bones from the rabbit their father had left for them. There was no meat left, but they were good to chew on. "What did you do with those bones, Arnya?" he asked.

She pointed. "They were there, on that rock." Something must have taken them – something that wasn't as scared of fire as other animals were.

Peli stared into the darkness. "A wolf?" he whispered. He searched for footprints, but the fire didn't give enough light. He tossed more wood into the flames and hoped that they would be safe until morning.

Peli crept closer to the fire, made himself a comfortable hollow in the earth, and shut his eyes. Happier times, when they lived with the other families, came to him in his dreams. He was six years old again and climbing trees and chasing birds with his friend Gil. At night, around the fire, they had watched the men act out the day's hunt. Peli moaned in his dreams and rolled around as he saw his father hold the head of a bison high above his own head and dance through the firelight to chanting voices.

His uncle, alive in the boy's dream, stalked the make-believe bison and pretended to kill it with his lance. "Look out!" Peli wanted to shout at his father, afraid he would be hurt.

Suddenly, he was jolted awake by a burning pain. He had rolled too close to the fire. He sat up and put a blistered finger into his mouth. Tears of anger filled his eyes. He was angry that they had left their friends, angry that drought had driven away the animals, angry that his father hadn't taken him on the hunt. But he was miserable, too, and afraid, because he and Arnya were alone. With every hour, it became clearer that something had happened to their parents and they might never return.

Peli hugged his knees and gazed out across the tops of the trees. The moon shone down, turning them into patches of brightness and splotches of shadow. Somewhere in the forest there had to be food, and not just berries or nuts. He wanted meat.

Curling up and lying down again by the fire, Peli remembered the young pig that his father and mother had caught this time last year. The roasted meat had smelled wonderful and tasted even better.

Arnya had been the first to hear the family of pigs grunting and squealing near the waterhole. Peli had to admit that his sister had sharper ears than anyone else. "But they're *my* pigs," she had complained loudly when she had to stay at the cave with Peli while her mother and father went after them. "I heard them first."

"What about me? I should be going hunting, not sitting with my little sister." Peli had picked up a handful of stones and aimed them, one at a time, at the boulder sticking out of the cliff. Surprisingly, he missed with only one – his best score yet.

Forgetting how cross he felt at having to stay behind, he had sneaked into the cave and got his father's second-best sling. The stone he threw with it hit a boulder so hard it smashed into little pieces. When his father saw what he could do, Peli told himself, he would have to take him on the next hunt.

But he didn't. Peli was again left behind to look after his sister, and his father was angry that the boy had used the sling without permission.

That was a year ago, and Peli still felt resentful. If his father had taken him hunting, maybe things wouldn't be so bad right now. If he had gone on this hunt instead of his mother...

But he wasn't thinking straight. It didn't matter who did the hunting, there was nothing to catch, and there wouldn't be until the animals came back to the waterhole.

As he turned over to warm his back at the fire, something hissed. He held his breath and listened. Another hiss... It was raindrops falling on the fire where it wasn't sheltered by the rock overhang. Peli looked blearily up at the sky. The moon had disappeared and there were no stars. It had already rained for three days and now it was raining again.

Would it be enough?

Chapter Three

Arnya woke to dark clouds and pelting rain. She ran outside, turned her face up to the sky, and held out her hands. "Rain," she shouted. "I love it!" She laughed as the water dripped from her hair and ran down her legs. "And listen!" She turned her head and stood like a rock.

"What is it?"

"Running water," she whispered. "Peli, it's the stream. There must have been lots of rain back there." She waved her hand towards the mountains, hidden under thick mist. "The pigs and deer will come back now. Then Mother and Father will come home – won't they?"

"Yes." Peli nodded slowly, but he knew she didn't believe him.

"You don't think they will." Arnya limped towards him and took his hand.

"I… I don't know."

"Why?"

"It has been raining for three days now."

"Well, I know *that*." Arnya sounded impatient. "It's more reason for them to come home."

"If they were coming back because of the rain, they should have been here two days ago."

"But they wouldn't go away and leave us – I mean really leave us!"

"Of course they wouldn't. Well, they wouldn't *mean* to. But what if something happened to them? What if they're…" He didn't want to say it.

"If they're what?" Arnya shook his arm.

"Hurt or something." He turned away from her, not wanting to show the fear in his eyes. Then he turned back. "You don't remember Father's brother, do you?"

Arnya shook her head.

Peli began telling her about the leopard.

As he finished his story, Arnya crouched and stared into the embers of the fire. "What are we going to do?"

Peli could hear the despair in her voice. He knelt beside her. That was the question he had been asking himself for the last three days. What were they going to do? Dejectedly, he stared into the fire, poking it with a stick. Sparks spat out at him. One landed on his foot.

"Ouch!" It hurt. He leaped up, grabbed an armful of last night's wood, and heaved it onto the fire. Smoke billowed into the air. "I'll tell you what I'm going to do!" He glared down at his sister. "I'm going to find some food – proper food. Are you coming?"

There were no nuts left on the tree that Arnya had found the night before, and that sort of tree was scarce. The children had to follow the winding tracks left by animals a long way into the forest before they found another.

"There's one," Peli shouted, pointing to a slender tree at the far side of a clearing. Nuts would be better than nothing, but the only nuts they could see were on the top branches.

"I'll go," Arnya said. "You're too heavy. You'll break the tree and we'll have no nuts next year."

If we're still alive next year, Peli thought, but he didn't say it. Anyway, Arnya was a very good climber. She might have a weak foot, but her arms and shoulders were strong. In seconds, she had scrambled high into the tree and was tossing nuts down to her brother.

"Only a few more," she called, reaching up to the last branch. Then, abruptly, she stopped, turning her head to one side and then the other. Peli could tell she was listening to something, trying to decide where the noise was coming from. She held one hand behind her ear to trap the sound.

"Peli," she whispered down to him, pointing to the part of the forest where the undergrowth was thickest. "Over there."

Peli's gaze followed her pointing finger. "Something is in the bushes." He remembered the bones missing from beside the fire. What had taken them? Was it hunting him and his sister now?

Peli was already backing towards a large tree with low-hanging branches when Arnya's scream echoed through the forest. "Run, Peli! It's a boar!"

Leaping high, Peli hooked his fingers around a branch and grabbed it with the other hand. He swung himself into the tree just as the boar rushed out of the bushes and skidded to a halt beneath him. Its chisel-shaped feet, which looked too small to carry its huge body, left stab marks in the damp earth. Squealing with anger at being disturbed, it swung this way and that, searching for its enemy.

Peli stared down from his safe perch at a hunched back covered in coarse black hair, and small eyes slanting beneath floppy ears. Its curved tusks almost formed a circle from each side of its mouth. Peli reviewed all the things his father had told him about wild boars, but he hadn't mentioned that they ate rabbit bones!

"The boar is clever," his father had said. "And it is patient. When you get sick of the hunt, it will still be waiting for a chance to hunt *you*." With a pointed stick, he scratched the shape of the boar in the sand. "It looks clumsy, but it's as agile as a cat. And it's fast. You will never outrun it. There is only one thing it can't do and that is climb. Remember that. It could save your life."

The boar stamped around in the middle of the clearing, rooting at a patch of wet earth with its snout, flinging lumps of mud into the air and squealing and snorting. Suddenly, it stopped, backed up a little, and stared into the trees above.

Can it see this far? Peli wondered. His father hadn't said anything about that. The boar's snout waggled as it sniffed the air. Then it trotted to the base of Peli's tree, stood on its hind legs, and scraped at the trunk with its front feet. It snorted.

"Peli!" Arnya's frightened whisper floated through the trees. "What are we going to do?" The boar swung around and trotted towards the sound.

"We'll think of something." He couldn't guess what, but there was no point in telling his sister that. "We might have to wait until it gets tired of hanging around here and goes away." But when would that happen? Never, if what his father had told him was true. Certainly not until after dark, and then there would be other dangerous creatures in the forest – cats and wolves.

"I can't stay here much longer. This branch is going to break," Arnya called. "I'm coming over."

"No! Stay there. Don't climb down!" Peli was picturing Arnya running across the clearing and the boar catching her.

"No. I'm not getting down. I was going to climb through the treetops. They're all touching."

Although Peli couldn't see his sister, he could see the slender nut tree she had climbed. It had grown up in the shelter of two old trees with heavy

29

branches that stretched out on either side. Now the leaves of the nut tree quivered and were still. After that, Peli could follow Arnya's progress through the treetops by watching for swaying branches.

Then all movement stopped. Everything was quiet, except for the boar, snorting as it rooted among the fallen leaves for grubs and worms. Now and then, it stopped and sniffed the air. It's checking on us, Peli thought. He was growing both impatient and nervous – although he didn't want to admit it. "Where are you now?" he called.

"Up here." Arnya's mischievous face poked out from a leafy branch above him. She swung down to his side. "Do you want some nuts?" She tipped some from her bag into his cupped hands.

Arnya threw shells at the boar and laughed when it spun around squealing. She felt brave with it down there, unable to get her.

"No!" Peli grabbed her arm. "That won't help. We want it to forget about us and go away."

"All right," she grumbled. "But what's to stop *us* from going away from the *boar*?"

"*It* is! It would kill us if it caught us!"

"But what's to stop us from getting to the edge of the forest the way I got over here?"

"Through the treetops?"

"Of course."

"We couldn't go all the way like that. There must be some gaps."

"Maybe. But I'd rather try that than sit around here waiting for night to come. Especially as we don't know if it'll go away even then."

Peli was staring at his sister. This was not the frightened little girl who had complained about being cold and hungry. This Arnya was at home in the trees.

"Come on," she said, standing up. She grinned at him, and all at once he felt they could work things out together. Even if they *were* left on their own, it didn't have to be the end.

Chapter Four

"Remember that Father wasn't just trying to scare us when he told us how dangerous the boar is," Peli warned as they looked down.

Twice the animal had hooked into a tree root with its tusks. It squealed angrily and flailed about until it was free. Now it was resting on its belly on the churned-up earth, its head lying on its short front legs. Its eyes were shut, but Peli knew it wasn't sleeping. Now and then, the long snout twitched, an ear flicked, and it grunted.

"We have to be quiet or it will follow us."

"We won't make a sound," Arnya whispered. She edged along a strong branch until she disappeared among the leaves.

Peli waited until he saw a slight movement in the next tree, then he followed. He chose branches that would take his weight and stepped along them sideways, holding onto anything he could reach.

They went from tree to tree without touching the ground until they were almost at the edge of the forest, but the trees were sparse there. Was the boar still dozing beneath the first tree, or was it following them silently on the ground?

"Stop," said Arnya suddenly. Peli had almost bumped into her.

"What's wrong?" he asked nervously.

She pointed to the next tree. It was smaller than the others they had crossed. Its branches were thin. They might support Arnya's weight, but Peli would go crashing to the ground.

Where was the boar? Peli leaned over, trying to see the ground through the thick blanket of leaves. The beast could be anywhere down there, and they would never know until it was too late.

He climbed down to the next branch. Now he could see small bushes and patches of earth. A breeze lifted some dead leaves, tumbled them over, and floated them back onto the damp earth. He waited. There was no sound. Nothing moved. He lowered himself onto another branch, the last thing between him and the ground.

How far was it to the next big tree? Thirty or thirty-five paces? One of its highest branches moved. Arnya was there already. Her strong arms had pulled her across easily.

Peli looked at the ground again. Should he leap down and race across the clearing? If the boar had followed, it would hear him.

Should he depend on silence, then, and not speed? Was there anywhere he could hide if the boar came at him before he reached the next tree? There was a big rock on the edge of the clearing, barely visible under a covering of creepers. If he stretched his arms up, he could reach the top of it, and the creepers would help. But what if the boar got to him first?

The more Peli thought about it, the more afraid he was to leave the safety of his tree, but he couldn't stay there forever. There was always the chance that the boar had given up and gone away. He looked around one last time, took several deep breaths, then slid quietly to the ground. He crept out of the shadowy undergrowth towards the tree, making a detour that would take him past the rock.

Less than halfway across, he heard Arnya's warning scream. "It's coming, Peli! Look out!"

Peli ran straight at the rock, but the boar charged across the clearing with such speed that Peli knew it would catch him. The gap was closing fast when a dark shape shot out of the bushes and fastened onto the boar's ear. A half-grown wolf had attacked out of nowhere!

The boar squealed and flung itself around until it had shaken free, giving Peli just enough time to scramble to safety on top of the rock. Behind him, the boar swung around and charged its attacker. The wolf, cornered against the rock, sprang up beside Peli, but the boar was going too fast to stop. It slid head first into the rock, smashing one of its gleaming tusks. Staggering back, it tossed its head, squealing with pain.

For a moment, the boy and the wolf remained motionless, like part of the rock. The boy looked into the wolf's pale brown eyes. It had saved him. He stretched out one hand to touch it. Then its lips curled back in a snarl, and the wolf leaped down behind the rock and disappeared.

Still shaking its head, the boar charged off in the opposite direction.

Peli couldn't move. He was frozen to the rock until Arnya's voice floated down from the tree.

"What was that?" she called.

"A wolf – I think." He could hardly believe what he was saying. "But where's the boar? Is it safe to get down?"

"It's gone. I can see it on the cliff above the river." There was a rustling sound and she landed on the ground beside Peli's rock. "Come on. It's not far to the cave. We don't have to go through the treetops any more."

Peli slid down from the rock. His legs shook, and he took Arnya's hand as they hurried out of the forest and scrambled up the path.

"Was it really a wolf?" she panted.

"A young she-wolf. She saved me. The boar would have got me if she hadn't gone for it."

"She might go for us next time! You know wolves are dangerous!"

"But not as dangerous as that boar," Peli insisted. "It's big trouble. If we don't get it, sooner or later it will get one of us. Anyway, it would be good to eat."

Back at the cave, Peli and Arnya sat around the fire, cracking nuts and talking about the wolf. "Do you remember that wolf two summers ago?" Peli asked. "It was with some men from the next valley."

Arnya nodded. "It didn't like us."

"It didn't like anyone – except its own people – but they said it was good for hunting. I wonder if this she-wolf would help us to hunt?"

"It would probably hunt *us*!" said Arnya.

Peli knew that Arnya didn't like wolves, but she hadn't been close to this one, as he had. "Anyway, what are we going to do about this boar?" he said, changing the subject. If she knew what he was thinking – that he would like to see the wolf again – she would make a fuss.

"Catch it in the bear trap?" Arnya suggested.

"We'd have to repair it first. The sides have caved in and we'd need to cut sticks for the top."

"We could do that."

"No. It would take all day. The boar would hear us and we might not be so lucky next time." We wouldn't have a wolf to help us either, he thought, as he poked a stick into the fire. When it flared up, he went further into the cave and lit a small torch.

"What are you doing?" Arnya demanded. She stood up and limped after him.

"I'm going to do what Father does before a hunt." Peli's voice echoed back at him from the rock walls.

From the shelf where his father kept his tools and weapons, Peli took a stone bowl, one of the most precious things they owned. Arnya looked horrified. "It's all right," he said. "We need it, and I'll put it back later."

Since the rain, water had been seeping through a crevice near the entrance. Peli held the bowl under the drips. When it was full, he walked back with it into the cave. "One, two, three, four…" He counted the paces on his fingers until he got to ten, and another ten, then he stopped. At this point, the cave divided into two narrow tunnels and the roof came down low over their heads.

Peli's father had brought him here once. They had crawled through one of the tunnels on their stomachs. The dust they had stirred up almost suffocated him, and he was terrified that the roof would fall down and crush them. Afterwards, he had frightened Arnya with stories about it.

"Do we have to go in here?" Arnya whimpered, clutching at the back of Peli's tunic.

"Of course we do. There's nothing to be afraid of. But, if you're too scared, you can wait here." Peli felt some confidence, because he knew what was at the other end, but he still dreaded going on by himself.

"Make up your mind. I can't wait any longer," he told her. Holding the torch out in front of him, and steadying the bowl in his other hand, he began crawling. Arnya followed so close behind him that her fingers often brushed against his feet.

Choking fumes from the bear fat filled the tunnel. There was no way out for the smoke, and it dimmed the light until it was useless. Peli tried to shield his head with one arm, but still he could barely breathe.

"I can't go… any further." Arnya's voice was a faint cry.

"Not far now," Peli encouraged her, wondering why it seemed much further than he remembered. Maybe it was taking longer because his father had been here often and had moved faster.

Or – maybe he had chosen the wrong tunnel! He had heard stories about caves that dropped into deep holes without warning. Stopping, he put down the bowl and reached out to scratch at the dusty floor ahead with nervous fingers. That part felt solid. Pushing the bowl ahead of him, he crawled a bit further and scratched around again. The torch crackled, and burning fat spattered onto his arm. He pulled back, inhaling sharply at the pain, and Arnya sobbed behind him. He had to go on.

Peli had gone no further than his own length before the flame flickered and curved away from him. The smoky fumes seemed less dense. A draught of air was coming from somewhere, and he could lift his head without bumping it on the rock above. He reached up. Nothing. Scrambling to his feet, he called, "We're through!"

Peli's voice was echoing around a high-roofed chamber. His torch lit the walls, but parts of the ceiling disappeared into shadow.

"What's that?" Arnya whispered fearfully.

A bison charged across the cave wall, chased by a hunter armed with a spear. A boar trotted across a rocky outcrop, its curved tusks threatening. Three deer leaped gracefully over a fourth deer. A herd of horses galloped furiously into the shadows. They all appeared to move in the flaring light. Terrified, Arnya backed away.

"Don't be frightened. They're not real. Come and see." Peli took her hand. She followed him unwillingly, keeping her head turned away from the parade of frightening beasts.

"Look at them," he whispered, remembering his own fear the first time he saw them.

Arnya edged out from behind him. "What are they? Where did they come from?"

"Father made them – all except that one." He pointed to a cat-shaped creature with a huge head and two immense teeth. It was partly hidden in a dark corner. "That was here when we came. It's very old and bits of it have come off, see?" He pointed to gaps in the outline where the rock had flaked away, taking the colour with it.

"What are they for?" Arnya's eyes were wide.

"To help with a good hunt. That's why we're here. If I make a picture of a boar on this wall, we're sure to catch that one before it gets us." Peli looked at the deer his father had painted before the last hunt. It was a good painting, but Peli's parents had tracked that deer for a long time and come back weary and empty-handed.

That's no way to think, Peli told himself angrily. Leaving Arnya staring at the painted wall, he went back for the bowl he had left by the tunnel.

On a narrow shelf were three piles of clay, one red, one white, and one black. Peli scooped up a handful of the black clay and stirred it into the water with a stick, until it made a thick paste.

"Are you going to make your boar just like the one Father made?" asked Arnya.

Peli stood in front of an empty space on the wall. He held the bowl in one hand and the stick in the other. He hesitated. He could draw the boar easily enough, but would that make a good spell? When his father had drawn the deer, it didn't work. Maybe he didn't get it right. How were they going to hunt this boar? They would never get it with a spear. It was too fast and too strong. They didn't even know where it was.

Their father had said that, because the boar was clever and fast and patient, it was the most difficult animal to hunt. "If I show it being speared, that wouldn't work, because even together we're not strong enough to do that," Peli said thoughtfully. "I have to make it something that is possible."

"What about when we were up in the tree and it was charging around underneath?"

"But it was after *us* then," objected Peli.

"What about after it crashed into the rock?"

"Yes. Maybe. That's where we saw it last."

"No it's not. Remember? I told you I saw it after that on the cliff above the river."

"So you did. Maybe if I show it on the cliff, that would help us find it. We can go back and follow its tracks from there." Peli dipped the stick into the bowl and drew two lines – one across and one down. "That's the cliff top. Now for the boar."

Chapter Five

When Peli had finished the boar, it stood with its back to the cliff edge. Two hunters faced it, one taller than the other.

"Is that me?" Arnya asked, pointing at the smaller one.

"Yes." Peli added a line sticking up from the small hunter's hand. "And that's your torch."

Arnya nodded. "Put a torch in my other hand, too. Fire is the only thing boars are afraid of."

"Good idea." Peli added another line.

"What about its broken tusk?"

Peli frowned as his stick hovered around the boar's head. He had already coloured the head black. If he drew the tusk, black on black, no one would see it. It was important to get everything right, or the magic wouldn't work.

His frown cleared. He put down the bowl and the stick. Then he gathered a mouthful of saliva, spat into his hand, and added a pinch of red clay. Using his finger, he dabbed the red colour onto the boar's mouth. "There! That's the tusk it broke." He stepped back, feeling pleased with himself, then reached up and dabbed more red on the boar's ear. "And that's where the wolf got it."

"Is that all?" Arnya was sitting down to rest her foot. She was tired.

"One last thing," Peli said. Picking up the torch, he went to a corner hidden in the shadows. Arnya scrambled up and followed him. The torchlight shone on a heap of hairy animal skins. Peli took one corner and lifted it up. Underneath was a pile of gleaming bones.

"What is it?" Arnya shuddered.

"Hold this." Peli gave her the torch while he picked up a boar's skull. Tusks curved from each side of its jaw to make a complete circle.

"What do we want that for?"

"You'll see. I've got to carry this, so you go first and carry the torch. Get going."

Arnya was scared of going back through the tunnel. She couldn't forget the feeling that the

46

mountain was pressing down on her body. She couldn't forget the suffocating dust.

"I don't want to," she whimpered. "What if we get stuck halfway? We'd die there."

"We'll die here if we don't go," said Peli, trying to reason with her. "Anyway, Father has been in and out of here many times. If he didn't get stuck, we won't."

"And there's no other way out?"

For a moment, Peli thought of the cool air that came into this part of the cave. He had felt it when he was here before and had meant to ask his father about it. Now it was too late. "No, there's no other way."

Arnya turned away from him. She raised the torch high and crept towards the patch of darkness that was the beginning of the tunnel.

Holding the torch out in front, she wriggled forward on her belly. Without Peli's feet in front, disturbing the dust, breathing was easier, and she tried to forget the weight of the mountain above.

"We're nearly there, Peli!" she called at last. Light was coming in from the outside and she could see the shapes of the rocks. "Peli?"

He didn't answer. Arnya slithered through the opening, stood up, and turned around.

"Peli!" She shouted into the tunnel. Still no answer. What had happened? Surely he couldn't be stuck! She would have to go back. Pushing the torch ahead, she crawled back into the tunnel, pulling herself along on her elbows.

She guessed she must be about halfway through when she thought she heard Peli calling. "Arnya?" She stopped. His voice was so faint. "Arnya?" She heard it again.

"Peli! Where are you?"

"I'm here, but I'm stuck. It's the boarskin. It's got tangled in the skull somehow."

"Go back then."

"I can't do that either. It's jammed."

Arnya wriggled forward a short distance and found herself touching a patch of coarse hair. It was the boarskin. She tugged and pulled at it as Peli pushed from the other side. It moved a little, then jammed again on something up by the roof. She ran her fingers around the edges, feeling the narrow jawbone inside the skin.

"Let it go," she said, scraping the earth away from underneath. "I'll try to free it." Grabbing hold of the skull up near the roof, she wriggled it from side to side. It came loose suddenly, smothering the torch and leaving her in darkness.

Arnya's return journey was slow and frightening, wriggling backwards and pulling the skin and the skull as Peli pushed. It could jam again at any moment. Arnya kept her eyes closed and pretended that it wasn't really dark. She didn't open them until she couldn't touch the rock above her head.

"I'm out," she cried. Peli felt the bundle pulled away from him as fresh air and daylight flooded in. He scrambled out and stood up beside her.

"It'll be dark soon," Peli said, setting the skull on a stone beside the fire and draping the skin over it so that the legs hung down in the right places. It almost looked alive!

"What are we going to do with it?"

"The hunting dance, of course – when it gets dark. That will help us catch our boar."

Chapter Six

"That hurts!" Peli yelped as Arnya tried to balance the boar skull on top of his head.

"Wait! I'll get something to stop it digging in." She picked four large, soft leaves from a tree near the cave and used them to pad the places where the bones were sharp. "Is that better?"

"I think so." Peli didn't want to nod, in case the skull fell off. "We'll put the skin under it. That will help to hold it on." Peli crouched down and Arnya draped the skin over him, wrinkling her nose at the smell, then replaced the skull on his head.

With two legs hanging down in front and two behind, and the tusks curving out from each side of the jaw, Peli could have been a real wild pig. In the firelight, with the darkness closing in around them, it looked scary. It was worse when he swung his shoulders and spun around, first one way and then the other, squealing and tossing his head.

Peli trotted around the fire, in and out of the shadows, copying the hunting dance he had watched his father perform. He had just reached the spot where the ground fell away steeply when something sprang on him from beyond the firelight, snarling and tearing at the boarskin.

"Wolf!" Arnya screamed.

Peli rolled away, dropping the skin and almost sliding over the cliff as he scuttled across to crouch beside his sister. They watched the wolf savage the skin, ripping out mouthfuls of bristly hair.

Arnya grabbed a burning stick from the fire and shook it at the wolf. The snarling beast backed away a few steps, but a line of hair still stood up on her spine and her ears lay flat against her head.

Peli grabbed Arnya's arm as she raised the stick again. "No," he whispered. "Just watch."

The wolf lifted her head, and boy and wolf were staring into each other's eyes for the second time. It seemed forever before the wolf dropped her gaze, turned around, and trotted down into the bushes.

"It was trying to kill a dead boarskin!" Now that the wolf had gone, Arnya giggled nervously.

"Maybe she was trying to tell us something," suggested Peli.

"Well, I've had enough of wolves and hunting dances." Arnya gathered up the remains of the skin and the skull and sat by the fire. "I'm hungry."

"I'm sick of nuts," Peli complained as he cracked some on a stone. "I want meat." He chewed the nuts slowly as another thought occurred to him. "I feel sorry for that wolf, though. Did you see how skinny she was? She looked as if she hadn't eaten for days."

"She'd like to eat *us*!" Arnya glanced over her shoulder towards the shadows. "She might come when we're asleep and the fire dies down."

"I don't think she'd hurt us."

"She stole our rabbit bones!"

"That's different. But, if you're frightened, we'll take turns keeping watch. You can sleep first."

"You'll stay awake and look after the fire?"

"Of course I will."

Arnya hugged her bearskin around herself and curled up close to the flames. In no time, her breathing grew slow and steady. She was asleep.

After all that had happened that day, Peli was exhausted, too. He didn't dare lie down in the warmth or make himself comfortable, so he poked a few sticks into the fire and leaned back against a boulder. To keep awake, he made himself stare in turn at the fire, and into the shadows where the wolf had disappeared.

A draught of cold air chilled his bare arms. He slid lower and closed his eyes against the stinging smoke that drifted towards him. His head tilted sideways and now his eyes remained closed.

In his dream, Peli had climbed up the hill from the forest. Snow covered the open ground and clung to the trees. A large group of strangers sat around the fire and there was no room for him. He crouched in the shadows, shivering with cold. A woman came towards him on her hands and knees. She wrapped him in fur and took him close to the fire. Although he grew warmer, one shoulder remained outside the fur, and he dreamed that he was pulling it up around his neck.

Peli's eyes flicked open. A threatening growl had woken him. The wolf lay beside him, her muzzle and bared teeth no more than a hand's width from his face. His fingers were living out his dream and tugging at the thick fur around her neck.

Carefully, Peli took his hand away. A sudden movement and the wolf might attack! Now the growling began to diminish. The wolf stared at him, then blinked and laid her head on his shoulder.

Peli's arm had gone numb with the weight of the wolf pressing down on it. He wanted to pull it away, but he didn't dare. Through her hairy coat, he could feel her ribs against his. She was so thin. Cautiously, he let his hand creep towards her and touch the coarse hair on her shoulder – she didn't move – then on up to her ears, soft under his stroking fingers. She tensed and bared her teeth, but there was no growling. He hesitated, then continued petting her ears.

"It's all right, it's all right," he whispered, over and over. "I'm your friend." Slowly, the tension slackened and the young wolf sighed and closed her eyes. Peli slept, too.

It was dawn when he woke again. The wolf had gone. Peli sat up, cold and stiff, feeling that he had lost something of great value. Had the wolf been part of his dream? He rubbed his chest where he remembered her lying. Coarse dark hairs stuck to his hand. She was no dream!

The crackle of fresh sticks thrown onto the fire woke Arnya. "Do you think I'm not old enough to keep watch?" she grumbled.

"Of course I don't."

"Then why didn't you wake me? You need sleep, too, if we're going to get that boar today." She looked at him suspiciously. "You *did* sleep! That's why you didn't wake me."

Peli nodded sheepishly and stirred the fire.

"I'll never trust you again!" cried Arnya. "We're lucky the wolf didn't come. You said yourself she was hungry!"

"She *did* come."

"She might have killed us!"

"Well, she didn't. She came and lay beside me. She kept me warm."

"Where is she now?" asked Arnya.

Peli shrugged. "I don't know. When I woke up, she had gone. Anyway, forget that. We have to get into the forest and start looking for the boar."

Preparations for the hunt took some time. Arnya sorted through the store of cutting stones. "We'll need sharp ones. Pigs have got tough skins."

"Let me see." Peli examined the four she had chosen. He tried out each stone flake, the rounded part nestling in his palm. He sliced the sharp edge across the boarskin he had used for the hunting dance. Three of the flakes cut through easily. "This one's no good," he said, tossing the fourth back into the pile. "I couldn't cut my finger on it."

"These are the best we've got," said Arnya. "Father took the rest." She put the good ones into her bag and tied it around her waist, along with a deerskin for extra warmth.

Peli searched the ground near the cave entrance for pebbles to fit in his sling. He filled his pouch and tied it around his waist. Next, he tied carrying thongs halfway along the shafts of two spears. The points had been shaped with a flake and hardened in the fire by his father. Peli hoped they would be sharp enough to pierce the skin of a boar. He put one over his shoulder and gave the other to Arnya. Then, from a high shelf inside the cave, he took the last four torches.

"We can't take them all!" Arnya was horrified.

"Do you want to be in the forest with no fire to scare off that boar? We'll only light one of the torches to begin with. Then, when we find the boar, we'll light the rest."

Peli made himself sound positive, but at the back of his mind was the fear of what would happen to them if they didn't track the beast and kill it. Nuts were getting harder to find, and they needed meat. Arnya used to have a plump, round face, but now it was thinner and there were dark patches under her eyes. If they didn't get meat soon, they would be too weak to catch anything.

"Hold these." Peli gave Arnya two torches. He thrust another into the fire and held it there until the fat-soaked bark began to flare. "Come on." He headed down the path towards the forest.

When they reached the first trees, Peli looked back. They were hunting a dangerous animal that could finish up hunting them. Would they ever return to the warmth and safety of the cave? He stared into the bushes near the fire, hoping he might see the wolf, but nothing moved.

"Go quietly," he said to Arnya as he turned and led the way into the trees.

Chapter Seven

Silence was important, but so was speed. The oily smoke from Peli's torch curled through the trees behind them as they hurried along the forest tracks. There was no discussion about the way they should take. The cave painting showed the boar on the cliff, so that was where they must go. They came out of the trees about twenty paces from the edge.

"Wait there," Peli whispered, handing his flaring torch to his sister. He crawled forward until he was looking down into the river. Yellow water, stained with clay, tumbled over boulders, swirling into deep pools. Directly below, on a sandy beach, was a jumble of rocks that had broken away from the cliff. Peli edged back, nervous in case the ground he was lying on gave way as well.

"Peli!" Arnya screamed.

Peli swung around to see Arnya pressed against a tree, the burning torch held out at arm's length.

Crouched just beyond the flame was the wolf. The animal's bared teeth, flattened ears, and bristling hair showed that she intended to attack. A menacing snarl rippled from her throat.

"Keep still, Arnya." Peli stood up and walked slowly towards the wolf, searching for the words he had used to calm her by the fire.

With two paces to go, he stopped and reached out. "It's all right, Friend," he said, suddenly remembering. "It's all right."

The wolf's head turned. The growling died away. Peli edged sideways to stand beside Arnya.

"Now we've got two enemies," she whispered, "the wolf and the boar."

Peli shook his head and knelt down. "This one wants to be a friend." The wolf crawled towards him on her belly and sniffed his hand.

"She's not my friend," Arnya quavered.

"She will be. Give her time."

But there was no time. The wolf heard the noise in the bushes at the same time as Arnya, and long before Peli. "What is it?" he whispered when the wolf jerked upright, staring into the forest.

"It must be the boar." Arnya turned to him anxiously. "Shall we light the other torches?"

"Just one."

Arnya held the lit and unlit torches together. When the second one crackled and flared, she handed it to Peli. "Now what?"

They were alone again. The wolf had slunk off into the bushes and everything was quiet.

When they left the cave that morning, Peli had had no idea how they were going to kill the boar. He only knew that they had to start the hunt at the cliff. But, at that instant, a picture of what they must do flashed into his mind.

"We have to get the boar between us and the cliff. Then we can use the torches to scare it over the edge. Even if the fall doesn't kill it, it should be hurt badly enough for us to finish it off."

"Will that work?" Arnya sounded doubtful.

"Of course it will." Peli spoke confidently, but he knew it would take all the magic he had summoned with his cave painting and his dance. "Follow me. We'll sneak around behind it." Peli turned away so that Arnya would not see how scared he was, and crept further along the cliff before heading into the trees.

A few steps further on, they came to a clearing. Something rustled on the far side. Peli put out a hand to hold Arnya back. The bushes shook and out trotted the boar. Peli looked frantically for a tree to climb, but the boar didn't appear to know they were there. The bushes moved again and now the wolf appeared, following the boar as it scampered across the clearing. In seconds, they had both disappeared among the trees. The boar made no noise and the wolf moved like a shadow.

"Where did they go?" Arnya whispered.

Peli shook his head. "I don't know. But we can't stay here. They could come up behind us and we wouldn't know until it was too late. You climb that tree. You might be able to keep track of them from up there."

Peli took Arnya's torches and watched her swing up through the branches. She was out of sight in no time. He envied the way she climbed and the strength she had in her shoulders. "Can you see them?"

"Not yet." Her voice floated down through the canopy of leaves. Then, "Yes! I can see them both! They're upriver, close to the bank."

The tree shook as she slithered down. "Come on." She grabbed her torch. "We'll have to head them off and turn them back towards the cliff!" She slid into the bushes and made off at an angle towards the river.

Peli wished they could go faster, but he kept getting his spear tangled in the branches. The lit torch was a problem, too. At last, they arrived at the river bank. It sloped gently here. There was no steep cliff, and no boar either. Arnya looked disappointed. "We've lost it."

"Wait." Peli knelt down. "It's been here." He ran his fingers over footprints jabbed into the damp earth. "The boar came out of the forest and made for the river. It was trying to cross to the other side." He stood up, took a few steps towards the water, and bent down again. "And here I can see where the wolf headed it off. She's still with it, and they're making for the cliff. Come on!" He set off at a run.

Peli followed the tracks that zigzagged along the river bank. They went past the highest point on the cliff and then turned off into the forest. "Not again," he said angrily. "We're going around in circles! Can you see anything, Arnya?"

There was no answer. The silence behind him made Peli turn around. Arnya wasn't there. He should have waited. With her bad foot, she couldn't run as fast as he could, and she got tired easily. He would have to go back. He had taken only a few steps when she limped around the last bend.

"It's all right, Arnya. No need to hurry. We've lost them somewhere in there." Peli was waving towards the trees when, with a sudden crash of breaking wood, the boar erupted from a patch of bush halfway between him and his sister, with the wolf right behind.

Nearer now, the boar altered course and began to head for Arnya. She pushed the flaming torch towards it and tried to free her spear from the thong that fastened it to her back, but the boar was not going to stop. Peli knew with a sickening certainty that he was too far away to help.

It was the wolf that made the difference. She dived forward, nipping at the boar's hind leg. It squealed, spun around, and charged at her, slicing with its splintered tusk. The wolf yelped, but she didn't run. She dived past the tusk and grabbed the flopping ear. The boar swung this way and that. It spun and corkscrewed. Peli saw blood dripping from the wolf's shoulder, but she held on.

Peli knew that, without help, the wolf would lose the fight. Dreading what might happen then, he loosened his spear and launched himself into the battle, spear in one hand, torch in the other. From the corner of his eye, he saw Arnya creeping up from the other side.

He didn't know whether the boar was frightened by the torches, or whether it was so furious with the wolf that it didn't understand its danger, but, suddenly, it charged out onto the cliff. There was a rattle of stones and rocks breaking loose. Both wolf and boar disappeared.

Peli crawled out on the cliff edge as far as he dared. With one hand clutching a small tree, he peered over. Something black and hairy lay on the sandy river bank, almost covered with fallen rocks. He couldn't tell whether it was the boar or the wolf.

"Be careful," Arnya wailed behind him. "What can you see?"

Peli crawled back towards her. "I'm not sure. We'll have to go down."

Peli led the way along the cliff until they reached a track down to the river. There was the rock fall, but where was the thing he had seen from the cliff? Peli looked up. Was it safe to go any further? Were any more rocks going to come down? He would have to risk it.

"Wait there," he told Arnya, and clambered over the rock fall while she rested by the river.

Lining himself up with the tree at the top of the cliff, Peli crept forward until he was looking down on a black shape half-hidden beneath the rocks.

"Let it be the boar," he whispered as he rolled away the first rock. There was the splintered tusk and one eye partly hidden beneath a floppy ear. Peli had been holding his spear ready, but there was no need. The boar was dead. Peli should have been shouting with joy. The hunt had ended just as they had planned. Well, not quite.

Peli stared at the heap of rocks, trying to see into the gaps and crevices between them. The wolf had disappeared.

Chapter Eight

It was almost dark before they lit a fire among the rocks and got started on the boar. "It's too heavy to carry back to the cave, and something will steal it if we leave it here," Peli had said. "We'll have to stay with it."

He pictured the big cats that sometimes roamed up and down the river. He tried not to think about the wolf. He would gladly have shared the meat with her.

As the fire shot flames into the air, they spread the cutting stones out on a flat rock.

"Help me," said Peli. He grabbed one front leg, Arnya took hold of the hind leg, and they tipped the boar onto its back. Peli kicked a rock under its shoulder to stop it rolling onto its side again. Now he chose the sharpest flake and, standing astride the body of the boar, he slashed fiercely at the skin on its belly.

"It's tough!" he grunted, cutting again and again before the skin opened, revealing the warm flesh inside. Peli had helped to cut up many carcasses after successful hunts. He knew where to find the parts that were tender enough for a hungry hunter to eat without cooking. He pushed his hand in through the gap and pulled out the dark red liver. The first slice he gave to Arnya, but the second he kept for himself. It tasted delicious. It was like magic the way it returned strength to their bodies after days of starvation.

"More?" Arnya held out her hand.

"Soon. Our bellies can't manage too much good food at once. We'll have some more after we've got this skin off."

Arnya hooked her fingers onto the edge of the slash that Peli had already made. As he sliced the skin away from the flesh, she pulled.

The moon and the flames were making strange shadows along the river bank by the time they had finished. The skin was stretched out on the sand and held in place with heavy stones. Exhausted, they sat close to the fire, their arms wrapped around their knees. Arnya's mouth drooped. "I wish Mother and Father were here," she murmured, a tear squeezing down her cheek.

"So do I." Peli stood up slowly. The work wasn't done yet, and his body ached with weariness. Picking his way back between the rocks, he chose a young tree with thin branches and tore some away from the trunk. Back at the fire, he formed them into an arch over the flames and laid strips of meat across them, throwing leaves onto the ashes underneath. Smoke billowed up. "There," he said, "that will dry the meat and stop it from going bad." Wearily, he headed back down the river bank for more leaves.

Halfway there, Peli stopped. He could hear something. If Arnya had been with him, she would have known what it was. Was it a scratch of claws on rock? Or was it only water rippling over stone? Peli tried to force his ears to take in the sounds and sort them out. He looked around, wishing he had the eyes of the night animals. He was sorry he hadn't brought a torch. He had thought about it for a moment, then decided not to bother. He wasn't going more than thirty paces. He would have leaves to carry back, and he was so tired.

The noise came again. With his back to the river, he stared into the darkness at the foot of the cliff. Two points of light glowed briefly and disappeared.

"Eyes," he whispered, wondering if one of the big cats had smelled the meat. He edged back into the water. Some of the cats would swim if they had to, but they would think twice before following him into the river. He waded back to camp.

"Arnya!" said Peli, shaking her awake. "I saw something out there. I've come back for a torch. Stoke the fire and stay awake!"

Peli jammed a torch into the fire and waited until it flared. Holding it above his head, he took slow steps along the river bank, stopping at the place where he had heard the noise. He leaned forward, staring into the shadows. Almost beyond the reach of the light, there was a shape that didn't belong. Peli edged closer. He made out a tail and a body. He knew it was the wolf.

Peli hurried across the sand and knelt beside her. She was so still, he was sure she was dead.

Then he saw her ribs rise and fall. He jammed the torch upright in the sand. "It's all right, Friend," he whispered, and stroked her head. But it wasn't all right. Her eyes stayed shut and she didn't move.

Down at the river, Peli made a cup from his hands, scooped up some water, and hurried back. "It's all right, Friend," he told her again, and trickled the water into the corner of her mouth. There was a choking sound as she tried to cough. The water had got into her lungs. She shuddered and lay still again.

Peli knelt down and gently pushed his hands underneath her. Although she was so thin, she was heavy, and he struggled to pick her up. Her head hung to the side, her mouth fell open, and her tongue lolled out. Was she going to die?

In spite of being told to stay awake, Arnya was sleeping by the fire, wrapped up in the deerskin, as Peli staggered up. He laid the wolf beside her, and lay down himself. Stroking the soft ears, he talked to her until he fell asleep as well.

During the night, a rasping noise woke him. It was a leopard. He recognized its harsh purring cough. It could smell the meat. The fire had died down to a pile of embers, so it was a wonder that it hadn't come closer. Peli stood up and heaped more wood on the fire. Flames leaped into the air. The leopard bounded away into the darkness.

Perhaps the smell of the wolf had helped to keep the leopard at a distance, Peli thought, as he lay down again. That would have made it cautious. It didn't know that the poor thing was as good as

dead. He glanced across at the wolf and his heart leaped. Her eyes were open. She was watching him.

Peli fetched more water, this time in a piece of boarskin he had folded to make a bowl. He supported the wolf's head and shoulders with one arm and held the bowl in his other hand. Three times her tongue licked at the water, but he couldn't tell if she had swallowed. Then her eyes closed and he laid her back on the sand.

Leaving the bowl in front of her, Peli lay on his back, staring up at the stars. He wondered what was going to happen tomorrow, and the day after, and the day after that.

Today's hunt had been successful, but Peli knew they had been lucky, very lucky. He reached a hand out to the wolf and stroked her ears. They had been especially lucky to have the wolf to help them. She had saved their lives.

Chapter Nine

The early morning sky was pale the next time Peli woke. Arnya was still sleeping, so she couldn't have disturbed him. He turned his head. The wolf was struggling to sit up. Peli rolled over and supported her.

"It's all right, Friend," he said softly. Reaching for the water, he held it to her muzzle. She lapped fitfully, then lay down again. "I've got something you'll like better than that," he whispered to her. With a flake, he sliced off a lump of liver, cut it into small pieces, and offered them to her.

"You're giving our good meat to the wolf!" Arnya had woken up and seen what he was doing.

Peli fed her the last piece. "She's hungry."

"That's stupid! You'll feed her up until she's strong enough to attack us!"

"If she was going to attack us, why didn't she do it before?"

Arnya scowled.

"Don't you understand? If it hadn't been for her, the boar would have got me in the forest and you on the cliff!" Peli was getting impatient with his sister.

A threatening growl came from the wolf's throat. She struggled to get up, but staggered and collapsed onto the sand.

"It's all right, Friend," Peli said, crouching beside her and glaring at Arnya.

"She might be your friend, but she hates me." Arnya sniffed.

"Then you'd better do something to make her like you," Peli said, "because I'm keeping her."

"What can I do? I can't get near her."

"Feed her. That'll do for a start."

Arnya picked up a strip of the dried meat and edged towards the wolf, while Peli held onto the ruff of coarse hair around the animal's neck. She sniffed at the food, but didn't touch it.

"Put it down and move away," Peli suggested. When Arnya did that, the wolf reached out and gulped it down.

"Her leg looks bad." Arnya pointed at the wound made by the boar's tusk. The hair was matted and the shoulder was swollen. "That's why she couldn't stand up."

"What can we do about it?"

"Put some of Mother's special leaves on it, maybe. But I don't know if they'd work with a wolf." At the thought of saving a wolf, instead of killing it for its skin, Arnya's lips curled. It was almost funny. But then, since their parents had left, all the rules had been turned upside down. Arnya had to help with the hunting, and here was Peli wanting to know about healing.

"Where do these leaves grow?" he asked her.

"Near the cave. But we can't both go back there and leave the meat. Something will get it."

"I'll go back," said Peli. "You stay here."

"I'm not staying here with her," Arnya nodded at the wolf, "and you don't know what the leaves look like. And, before you suggest it, I'm not going back through the forest on my own either."

Arnya was right. They had to stay together. A moment later, he had decided what to do.

"Help me cut the carcass into smaller bits," he said. "We can hide most of it under different rocks. If that leopard comes, it won't have time to steal all of it. Anyway," he patted the wolf, remembering how her smell had kept the big cat away the night before, "you'll stand guard, won't you?"

The wolf sniffed at the meat he offered her, but this time she didn't eat. Something bad had got into her body through the cut. They had to find those leaves soon.

"Now for the rest of the meat," he said, cutting the boarskin in half. He wrapped two more pieces in each bit of skin. Using the spear thongs, he tied the smaller bundle onto Arnya's back and took the larger one himself. Arnya lit the last torch and they headed for the cave.

The sun was directly overhead by the time they came out of the forest and climbed the zigzag path. Remembering the bear that had taken over the cave when they left it once before, they approached carefully, and made sure it was empty.

Peli stowed the meat on a high ledge and lit a fire near the entrance. Arnya gathered her leaves.

"That'll keep hungry big cats away," said Peli, admiring the blaze. He added a few more sticks and they turned back towards the river. As they followed the forest paths, he wondered when they would return. How long would the fire keep the meat safe? How long before Friend could walk?

They found footprints along the river bank. They belonged to the leopard, Peli decided, but it had been wary of coming any closer to their camp.

Arnya soaked some leaves until they were mushy and handed them to Peli. "You do it," she muttered stiffly.

"It's all right, Friend," Peli whispered to the wolf, but he knew it wasn't. As he gently pressed the leaves onto the wound, her eyes remained shut and her breathing came in noisy gasps.

"You'll have to tie the leaves on," Arnya told him. It sounded easy, but soon Arnya had to help. They used strips of the boar's skin.

The moon was rising as the exhausted pair stoked the fire, raked out a few embers, and held bits of meat above them on sticks. After they had eaten, Peli took water and food to the wolf. She drank a little, but didn't eat. Arnya busied herself preparing fresh leaves.

"Lie still," Peli whispered as they tied them over the wound.

The wolf woke Peli the next morning. She was sitting up, gnawing at the strips of skin that kept the leaves in place. "You're better," he said, helping her remove the last of them. He began stroking her ears, but she pulled away.

"It worked?" Arnya sat up, rubbing her eyes.

"Yes, but..." The wolf was growling. She limped a few steps along the river bank.

"She can hear something," Arnya whispered. "So can I. Up there." She looked up at the cliff top. A handful of stones rattled down.

"Peli? Arnya?" A familiar voice called their names. The wolf's ears pricked in alarm, and she disappeared downriver.

Chapter Ten

"The rivers came up after the rain," their father explained as they sat by the fire eating. It was the first meat their parents had tasted since before they left. "That was why we couldn't get back."

"We should never have gone," their mother said. "We worried about you all the time, and we had no luck with the hunting."

"We were all right," Peli said. The good food of the last two days was making him forget the bad times. He hesitated to talk about the wolf. His father might say that he should have killed her for her skin. Anyway, she had run off. He felt sad about that, but they were lucky to have their parents back. Maybe hoping for the wolf as well was too much to ask for.

"I can see you did just fine without us." His father grinned proudly and sunk his strong yellow teeth into the boar meat.

Later that day, they packed the rest of the meat onto their backs and set off for the cave. They were climbing the zigzag path when their father suddenly stopped. "What's that?" Everyone turned to look. "Down there." He pointed towards a shadow moving among the bushes below.

Peli turned back on the path and began to call softly. "It's all right, Friend." The wolf limped towards his outstretched fingers. With one hand stroking her head, he told his parents how the wolf had attacked the boar and saved them from injury or even death.

"And I fixed her shoulder with some of your special leaves," Arnya told her mother.

That night, as they sat by the fire, their father told them stories about other wolves. "A tame wolf is a great thing to have," he said. "But this one might always have a limp."

"I don't know if that matters much," Peli said with a grin. "Arnya's got a limp, too, and there's nothing wrong with her."

From the Author

Stone Age people are sometimes pictured as uncaring and unintelligent. But have you ever tried to dig a hole large enough to trap a bear, using only sticks and your hands? Have you tried to catch wild animals for food and make clothes from their skins, or to make tools and weapons that really work, when stones and sticks are all you've got?

As a teacher, I have always found children keen to learn about families from those times. Some even say they would have liked to live then. So I decided to write this story about Arnya and Peli, two children who find themselves unexpectedly left alone, with only the shelter of their family's cave and a small fire.

Marie Gibson

From the Illustrator

When I was first offered the job of illustrating *A Friend in the Wild*, I knew it was just right for me. The subject of Paleolithic life has been a passion for me since I was first introduced to it at art school.

If I hadn't become a book illustrator, I would have liked to have been an archeological artist, but the nearest I have come to it is painting pictures for several books about ancient people and dinosaurs. Still, a few years ago, I actually did go on a search for dinosaur bones in central Queensland.

I used my youngest son and my niece, as well as my brother and his wife, as models for this book, and I had a lot of fun illustrating it.

Kelvin Hawley

Discussion Starters

1. Peli dreamed of happier times with the other families and his friend Gil. Do you think his dreams affected his behaviour towards the wolf? Which of them needed the other more?

2. Arnya's misshapen foot was an evil omen for the other families. Why would they think that? Do you think some families would have chosen to stay with the others, rather than face the extra hardship and danger of living alone?

3. Do you think you would be frightened, as Peli and Arnya were, of the paintings in the cave if you had never seen a drawing or painting before? Would you think they might have magical power?

4. Did Peli and Arnya prove themselves to be clever hunters, or were they just lucky? If their parents had never come back, do you think they would have continued to survive?